Published By Robert Corbin

@ Sean Turner

Dukan Diet: Your Path to Weight Loss

All Right RESERVED

ISBN 978-87-94477-36-9

TABLE OF CONTENTS

Shrimp And Avocado Salad 1

Rolls Of Smoked Salmon And Spinach 4

Piri Piri Chicken 7

Beef Kebabs 9

Zucchini And Lowfat Ricotta Cheese Casserole 11

Eggplant Caprese 12

Aromatic Roasted Roots 15

Ovenroasted Turkey 17

Strawberry Banana Smoothie 18

Basic Smoothie 20

Quick Chocolate Muffins 21

Egg Puff Muffins 23

Egg Custard Tart "Pastry" 25

Veal Scalondini With Cream Sauce 27

Tofu Breadsticks 29

Coriander Sole 31

Pancakes "Attack" According To Dukan 32

Lazy Khachapuri According 35

Pico De Gallo 39

Roasted Asparagus Prosciutto And Egg 41

Crispy Ginger Oat Biscuits 44

Hungarian Paprika Chicken 46

Skewered Bacon Ranch Chicken 49

Prime Rib With Garlic 51

Chicken Meatballs 53

Limekissed Shrimp 55

Oat Bran Galette 56

Quiche 58

Cheese And Garlic Chicken Pocket 59

Cheesy Broccoli Casserole 61

Super Breakfast Smoothie 63

Mushroom Tart 64

Vegetable Tart 65

Date Paste 68

Lemon Cornbread With Strawberries And Cream... 69

Rosemary And Garlic Chicken.................................... 72

Skewed Lemon Chicken With Dip............................. 74

Multiflavored Beef Attack 76

Octopus Salad With Cherry Tomatoes And Arugula 78

Eggplant Rolls With Cooked Ham And Cheese 81

Turkey Skewers With Peppers And Courgettes........ 84

Pan Fried Trout... 87

Salade Nicoise.. 89

Chicken Bruschetta... 91

Shrimp And Avocado Salad 93

Ham And Cheese Rolls 95

Blanched Brussel Sprouts With Crispy Ham 97

Dilled Fish Cakes 98

Butterfinger Pie 100

Watermelon Smoothie 102

Chocolate Pralines 103

Sweet & Sour Chicken 104

Steak Pizzaola 106

Regularity Muffins 109

Baked Bass 112

Suitable Protein Patty Soup 114

Endive And Caviar Salad 117

Easy Seafood Stirfry 118

Tea Cake With Goji Berries According 121

Muesli Bars In "White Chocolate" 125

Easy Herb Roasted Turkey 131

Roasted Okra 133

Pak Choi And Chicken Stirfry 134

Quick And Easy Chicken And Tomato 137

Melt In Your Mouth Baby Back Ribs 139

Dijonworcestershire Marinated Grilled Flank Steak
.... 141

Shrimp And Avocado Salad

Ingredients:

- 200 g of cooked and peeled shrimps
- 1 ripe avocado, peeled and diced
- 1 cucumber, diced
- 1 tomato, diced
- Juice of 1 lemon
- Extra virgin olive oil
- Salt and pepper
- Mixed salad leaves (e.g. lettuce, arugula, radicchio)
- Chopped fresh parsley (optional).

Directions:

1. In a bowl, combine the shrimp, diced avocado, diced cucumber, and diced tomato.
2. Squeeze the lemon juice over the shrimp and vegetable mixture to keep the avocado from oxidizing and mix gently.
3. Add a drizzle of extra virgin olive oil and season with salt and pepper to taste.
4. Mix the Ingredients: well to distribute the dressing evenly.
5. Arrange the mixed salad leaves on the bottom of a serving plate.
6. Pour the shrimp and vegetable mixture over the salad leaves.
7. If desired, sprinkle with chopped fresh parsley for a fresh note.
8. Serve Shrimp Avocado Salad immediately as a main course or light side dish.
9. Shrimp Avocado Salad is a healthy and tasty choice that is high in protein and healthy fats.

2. In a bowl, mix the spinach with the cream cheese. Add lemon juice, salt, pepper and herbs to taste. Mix well to obtain a homogeneous mixture.
3. Take a slice of smoked salmon and place a teaspoon of spinach and cream cheese filling on the end. Gently roll the salmon around the filling, creating a compact roll. Repeat process with remaining salmon slices and remaining filling.
4. You can serve the smoked salmon and spinach rolls as they are, or, if you prefer, you can wrap them in transparent film and place them in the refrigerator for at least 12 hours to make them compact and flavour.
5. Before serving, cut the rolls in half or into smaller pieces, depending on your preference.
6. You can garnish the rolls with thin slices of lemon or fresh herbs for an eyecatching presentation.

7. The smoked salmon and spinach rolls are ideal as a light appetizer or as a main course at a dinner party.
8. They fit well into the Dukan diet in later phases, such as the consolidation or stabilization phase, where smoked salmon, spinach, and light cream cheese are allowed.
9. Remember to adjust portions according to your dietary needs and specific Dukan Diet guidelines.

Piri Piri Chicken

Ingredients:

- 2 tbsp cider vinegar
- ½ tsp lemon juice
- ½ tsp lime juice
- Sea salt, according to taste
- Black pepper, ground, according to taste
- 2 chicken breast fillets, skinless
- 1 clove of garlic, finely chopped
- 1 tsp chili flakes, crushed
- ½ tsp paprika
- ½ tsp oregano

- Fatfree yogurt, according to taste

Directions:

1. In a bowl, prepare a marinade by mixing the garlic, chili flakes, paprika, oregano, cider vinegar and lemon juice together.
2. Place each piece of chicken in the marinade and coat the fillet thoroughly.
3. Cover this bowl with cling wrap and place it in the refrigerator overnight.
4. The next day, remove the chicken from the bowl and season with salt and pepper according to taste.
5. Grill on medium heat, till the fillets are thoroughly cooked.
6. Serve along with fatfree yogurt, after adding the lime juice to it.

Beef Kebabs

Ingredients:

- ½ tbsp cider vinegar

- 1 tbsp cooking oil

- Pinch of fresh thyme

- ½ bay leaf

- ½ lb beef fillet

- 2 tbsp lowsodium soy sauce

- 1 tbsp Dijon mustard

- 2 tbsp fresh lemon juice

Directions:

1. Cut the beef into largesized cubes evenly.

2. In a bowl, mix the soy sauce, Dijon mustard, lemon juice, vinegar, cooking oil, thyme and bay leaf to make a marinade with them.
3. Place the beef pieces in the marinade and make sure they are coated with it. Cover the bowl with cling wrap and keep it refrigerated for 34 hours.
4. Place the kebabs in an orderly manner and grill them till it is wellcooked, or how you prefer it.

Zucchini And Lowfat Ricotta Cheese Casserole

Ingredients:

- Grated light Parmesan cheese

- Salt and pepper (optional)

- 2 medium zucchini

- 200 g lowfat ricotta cheese

- 2 eggs

Directions:

1. Preheat the oven to 180°C (350°F). Grate the zucchini and squeeze them to remove excess water.
2. In a bowl, mix grated zucchini with lowfat ricotta and eggs. Add lightgrated cheese, salt, and pepper to taste and mix well.

3. Pour the zucchini and ricotta mixture into small, lightly greased cocotte or muffin molds.
4. Bake the zucchini and ricotta flans for about 25 to 30 minutes, or until golden brown on top and cooked in the center.
5. Let cool slightly before unmolding the flans. Serve the zucchini and ricotta flans as an appetizer.

Eggplant Caprese

Ingredients:

- 150 g buffalo mozzarella cheese

- Fresh basil

- Extravirgin olive oil

- 1 large eggplant

- 2 ripe tomatoes

- Salt and pepper to taste.

Directions:

1. Cut the eggplant into slices about 1 cm thick. Heat a grill or nonstick skillet.
2. Brush the eggplant slices with extra virgin olive oil and grill them for 3 to 4 minutes per side, until soft and lightly browned.
3. Slice the tomatoes and mozzarella into thick slices. Compose the Caprese by alternating a layer of eggplant, a layer of tomatoes, and a layer of mozzarella.

4. Add fresh basil leaves. Season with extra virgin olive oil, salt and pepper. Serve the eggplant caprese at room temperature.

Aromatic Roasted Roots

Ingredients:

- 1 celeriac
- 1 bulb garlic, halved
- 5 parsnips
- 5 carrots
- ½ swede (rutabaga)

Directions:

1. Preheat oven to 350°F.
2. Peel and cut all carrots and parsnips into quarters. Peel the celeriac and swede, and cut them into 1inch cubes.

3. Use an oil spray or 12 drops of oil inside a roasting pan to prevent the vegetables from sticking to pan.
4. Place garlic and vegetables into pan. Roast for about 5060 minutes or until the vegetables are tender.

Ovenroasted Turkey

Ingredients:

- 35 medium size shallots

- 2 tbsp. dried sage

- 1 whole turkey

- 1 tbsp. ground cumin

- 2 tbsp. dried sage

- Salt and pepper to taste

- Olive oil cooking spray

Directions:

1. Preheat oven to 375°F.
2. Combine ground salt & pepper, ground cumin, dried thyme & sage. Rub the spices gently into

the bird. You can use the cooking spray to oil the skin.

3. Cut shallots into quarters. Place turkey inside of a roasting pan. Place the shallots with the turkey inside a roasting bag. Add 1 tbsp. of water.
4. Using the bad allows you to use less fat to cook, thus saving on calories. Cook time depends on size of turkey.
5. About 2030min before the cooking time is up, cut open the roasting bag and let the brown a bit. At this time, check to see how much longer the turkey needs to cook.

Strawberry Banana Smoothie

Ingredients:

- 1 banana

- 1 cup almond milk

- 1 tablespoon honey

- 1 cup raspberries

- 1 cup strawberries

- 1 cup ice

Directions:

1. In a blender place all Ingredients: and blend until smooth
2. Pour smoothie in a glass and serve

Basic Smoothie

Ingredients:

- 1 cup coconut water
- 1 tablespoon honey
- 1 apple
- 1 pear

Directions:

1. In a blender place all Ingredients: and blend until smooth
2. Pour smoothie in a glass and serve

Quick Chocolate Muffins

Ingredients:

- 100 g fromage fraiche

- 1 teaspoon baking powder

- Sweetener, cinnamon, vanilla and 1 teaspoon cocoa powder

- 4 tablespoon oat bran

- 2 egg whites

- 50 ml vanilla yoghurt

- 2 tablespoon wheat bran

Directions:

1. It's all blended together and stir well with an electric mixer. executed in six muffins molds

bake 34 minutes in microwave oven put in plastic bag and place in refrigerator. may be frozen

Egg Puff Muffins

Ingredients:

- 3/4 cup egg whites

- Salt and pepper

- Mozzarella shredded cheese

- 3 eggs

- 1/2 cup frozen spinach, thawed

- Nitrite free turkey breast, low sodium is preferred

Directions:

1. Preheat your oven to 400F. Spray your muffin tin with nonstick spray, and push one slice of turkey into each muffin hole.

2. Mix eggs, egg whites, spinach, salt and pepper, and distribute evenly in each turkey hole. Then top with a small sprinkle of cheese.
3. Bake for 2535 mins, depending on how brown you want the muffins. Pop out and enjoy!!

Egg Custard Tart "Pastry"

Ingredients:

- Heat the milk in a sauce pan, add the oat bran and cook until thick, leave to cool a little.

- Egg custard.

- 2 eggs

- 1 cup of skimmed milk

- 1 level tbls sweetener.

- 3 tbls oat bran

- Half a cup of skimmed milk

- A little grated nutmeg.

Directions:

1. Powder a surface with a little corn flour, work the oat bran mixture into a ball and flatten slightly,
2. Put it into a oven proof dish or cake tin with sides, with your hands mould the "Pastry" around the tin and bake blind for 10 minutes. Gas mark 6
3. Whisk the eggs, milk, sweetener together and pour into the "pastry".
4. Sprinkle the top with ground nutmeg
5. Bake for 30 to 40 minutes (until the custard is set)

Veal Scalondini With Cream Sauce

Ingredients:

- 1 cup fatfree sour cream)

- 2 cups of trimmed green beans

- 14 oz. mushrooms

- 2 veal cutlets, cut 3/8 inch thick (about 6 oz. each)

- Salt and pepper to taste

Directions:

1. Wash, trim, and slice the mushrooms. In a nonstick saucepan, gently brown them until most of their moisture has gone and they begin to get tender.

2. Heat a nonstick frying pan large enough to hold the 2 veal cutlets. Gently brown them on both sides and remove from heat. Set aside.
3. In the same frying pan, place the sour cream, and heat on low heat, simmering and stirring constantly until it has reduced and has turned a golden color. Do not let it boil, or the sour cream will separate.
4. Pour into the saucepan with the mushrooms, and bring back to a simmer for 2 minutes. Season with salt and pepper to taste.
5. Steam the green beans in a separate saucepan.
6. Add the veal cutlets to the mushroom sauce, and continue simmering for 1 minute. Serve immediately with the green beans.

Tofu Breadsticks

Ingredients:

- 1 eggs
- 125 grams tofu
- 1 tsp. Yeast
- Salt
- Fresh rosemary
- Flavoring

Directions:

1. Preheat the oven to 180 degrees Celsius.
2. Blend the egg with tofu, yeast, a pinch of salt and rosemary. Mix until a dough forms.

3. Divide the dough into two parts. Add the pizza flavoring to one of the doughs and bacon flavoring to the other.

Coriander Sole

Ingredients:

- 3 tablespoons white wine (tolerated)
- 2 sprigs of fresh coriander
- 2 fillets of sole
- ½ lemon
- Salt and pepper

Directions:

1. Marinate 2 fillets of sole for 1 2 hours in a mixture of lemon juice and white wine in equal parts, seasoned with fresh coriander, salt and pepper.
2. Brown in a nonstick pan with the marinade.
3. Sprinkle with coriander before serving.

Pancakes "Attack" According To Dukan

Ingredients:

- 1 tbsp protein isolate 15 gr soy or whey
- 2 tbsp wheat gluten 30 gr
- 3 eggs
- 1/4 tsp soda
- 0.5 tsp vegetable oil
- 250 ml skimmed milk up to 1.5% fat
- 120 ml. Boiling water
- 2 tbsp oat bran 30 gr any grinding
- Sugar to taste
- A pinch of salt

Directions:

1. The cooking process is very simple and fast!
2. First you need to heat the milk. I do this with a microwave, set it to maximum power for a minute (I have 900)
3. Add bran to hot milk and stir well. Leave to swell for 510 minutes
4. Bran can be used in any grind, but I do not recommend bran flour in this recipe!
5. Add sifted gluten, isolate, a pinch of salt and sugar to taste to the bran
6. Knead well. You can do this manually. you can use a hand whisk
7. Add eggs to batter. Knead again until completely homogeneous, there should be no lumps.
8. At the very end, add soda and immediately pour boiling water. We mix.

9. It is no longer necessary to use a mixer, otherwise there will be a lot of bubbles we do not need this.
10. If there are still a lot of bubbles, let the dough stand for a while so that they disappear
11. Heat the pancake pan (I have D 22 cm). Pour half a teaspoon of oil into a heated frying pan and smear with a napkin. We do this only once at the very beginning.
12. Bake pancakes over medium heat as usual, 1.5 minutes on each side.

Lazy Khachapuri According

Ingredients:

- 2 eggs not very large

- 60 gr fatfree cheeseup to 7% fat(2 dops)

- 360 gr cottage cheesebetter from a pack, not grainy!

- 1 tsp baking powder10 gr

- 1 tsp frying oilsof necessity

- 2 tbsp cornstarch40 gr(2 dops)

- 2 tbsp oat bran30 gr

- Salt

- Greens to taste

Directions:

1. Cooking lazy khachapuri according to Dukan is very simple and takes a minimum of time! That's why they are "lazy"
2. To begin with, mix one egg with bran and leave to swell for ten minutes.
3. Three cheese on a fine grater, chop the greens
4. IMPORTANT! If you didn't find cheese with a fat content of less than 7%, but you really want khachapuri, you can take cheese a little fatter, but less than a gram, you should fit into 2 DOPs
5. We look at the fat content of cheese not in dry matter, but in BJU.
6. We calculate cheese according to the formula 210 / fat content of cheese \u003d gr \u003d 1 DOP
7. Let's look at an example. The fat content of cheese according to BJU is 12%. We calculate

according to the formula 210/12 \u003d 17.5 gr. It turns out 17.5 g of cheese with a fat content of 12% \u003d 1 DOP. So, in this recipe you can use 35 grams of cheese and a fat content of 12%, this will be 2 DOP

8. Mix all the Ingredients: until smooth, do not forget to add the second egg! (It is better to do this with a mixer) If your cottage cheese is not homogeneous, grind it separately until smooth
9. Let the dough rest for 10 minutes. During this time, it will thicken
10. Divide the finished dough into equal parts. Rolling koloboks
11. Choose the size of future khachapuri yourself, I make them small, the dough should not be sticky and easily form.
12. If your dough is liquid add a spoon of isolate or a spoonful of wheat bran, mix and leave the dough "rest" another five minutes

13. We form cakes from the bun and lay out in a hot frying pan
14. (First lubricate the pan with oil)
15. Fry under the lid over low heat on both sides until cooked
16. We put the finished lazy khachapuri on each other in a deep plate and cover with a lid or foil.
17. Fragrant and delicate lazy khachapuri are ready for Ducan!

Pico De Gallo

Ingredients:

- ½ jalapeno pepper, seeded and minced
- ½ lime, juiced
- 1 clove garlic, minced
- 1 pinch garlic powder
- 1 pinch ground cumin, or to taste
- 6 roma (plum) tomatoes, diced
- ½ red onion, minced
- 3 tablespoons chopped fresh cilantro
- 1 pinch salt and ground black pepper to taste

Directions:

1. Stir the tomatoes, onion, cilantro, jalapeno pepper, lime juice, garlic, garlic powder, cumin, salt, and pepper together in a bowl. Refrigerate at least 3 hours before serving.

Roasted Asparagus Prosciutto And Egg

Ingredients:

- 1 teaspoon distilled white vinegar

- 1 pinch salt

- 4 eggs

- ½ lemon, zested and juiced

- 1 pinch ground black pepper

- 1 bunch fresh asparagus, trimmed

- 1 tablespoon extravirgin olive oil

- 1 tablespoon olive oil

- 2 ounces minced prosciutto

- ground black pepper

Directions:

1. Preheat oven to 425 degrees F (220 degrees C). Place asparagus in a baking dish and drizzle with 1 tablespoon extravirgin olive oil.
2. Heat 1 tablespoon olive oil in a skillet over mediumlow heat. Add prosciuttocook, stirring, until golden and rendered, 3 to 4 minutes.
3. Sprinkle prosciutto and oil over asparagus. Season with black pepper and toss to coat. Roast in the preheated oven for 10 minutes.
4. Toss and return to oven until firm yet tender to the bite, 5 minutes.

5. Fill a large saucepan with 2 to 3 inches of water and bring to a boil over high heat. Reduce heat to mediumlow, pour in vinegar and pinch of salt.

6. Crack an egg into a bowl then gently slip the egg into the water. Repeat with remaining eggs.
7. Poach eggs until whites are firm and yolks have thickened but are not hard, 4 to 6 minutes.
8. Remove eggs from water with a slotted spoon, dab on a kitchen towel to remove excess water, then transfer to a warm plate.
9. Drizzle asparagus with lemon juice. Transfer asparagus to plates, top with poached egg and pinch of lemon zest. Season with black pepper and serve.

Crispy Ginger Oat Biscuits

Ingredients:

- 3/4 teaspoon ginger

- 1 teaspoon fat free yogurt

- 1/2 egg white

- 3 tablespoons of oat bran

- 2 tablespoons sweetener

- 1/2 teaspoon of baking powder

- 3 drops vanilla essence

Directions:

1. Preheat your oven to 180°C, 350°F or gas mark 4.

2. Place all the Ingredients: in a bowl and mix well with a spoon.
3. The mix should not be too runny (you may need to add a little extra oat bran but be mindful of your daily allowance!)
4. Spoon the mix out on to a silicon baking tray to make four biscuits (that way you can have 2 to make up 1 and 1/2 tablespoons of oat bran which is just right for Attack and to get to two tablespoons for Cruise you could just add the extra 1/2 tablespoon to a yogurt).
5. Bake for around 12 14 minutes.
6. If eaten warm they will be soft and if left to go cold they should go slightly crunchy.

Hungarian Paprika Chicken

Ingredients:

- 2 tablespoons of tomato paste/purée

- 2 tablespoons of sweet hungarian paprika

- 1 teaspoon of crushed red chilli pepper flakes

- 1 teaspoon of dried marjoram

- 1 cup chicken stock

- 1/2 cup reducedfat crème fraiche (tolerated item)

- 1 tablespoon of cornflour(corn starch) (tolerated item)

- 3 pounds of chicken pieces (with the skin removed but bone left in)

- 4 cups of finely diced onions

- 1 and 1/2 cups of assorted diced (bell) peppers

- 6 teaspoons of olive oil

- Sweetener/sea salt/freshly ground black pepper

Directions:

1. Fry the onion in a casserole dish until very soft, adding a little water if needed.
2. Stir in the (bell) peppers, tomato paste/purée, paprika, marjoram, crushed red chilli pepper flakes.
3. Add the chicken pieces and stir gently into the mixture.
4. Pour in the stock and place the lid on the dish and simmer on a low to medium heat until the chicken is tender.

5. Take out the chicken pieces and place them on a plate.
6. Add the crème fraiche and cornflour to the mix and stir continuously until the sauce coats the spoon.
7. Season with sea salt and freshly ground black pepper.
8. If a little additional sweetness is needed add a small amount of sweetener.
9. Put the chicken back into the sauce to reheat for a couple of minutes.
10. It is now ready to serve!

Skewered Bacon Ranch Chicken

Ingredients:

- 24 pieces of 1inch length red onions

- 4 skinless, boneless chicken breast halves cut into 1inch pieces

- 1 tsp hot Chile paste, like sambal oelek

- 1/3 cup ranch dressing

- 12 pcs of 6inch long bamboo skewer, soaked in water for 2 hours

- Pepper and salt to taste

- 12 slices of thick cut bacon

Directions:

1. In a large bowl, blend well hot Chile paste and ranch dressing. Toss in chicken to coat evenly, and allow to sit in the refrigerator for 13 hours.
2. Then, skewer chicken pieces and bacon by first threading in an onion, then one end of a strip of bacon into the skewer.
3. Then, add one chicken slice, and cover one side of chicken with baconthread bacon into skewer again.
4. Repeat this around 45 times by adding 45 amounts of chicken and threading the bacon alternately like a letter S. Then, repeat procedure until you have 12 skewered chicken and bacon.
5. Lightly oil the grate, and preheat grill to medium high fire.
6. Season with pepper, and salt the bacon/chicken skewers before placing on grill.

7. Grill each side for 34 minutes, or until meat is evenly browned and no longer pink. Remove from grill, serve, and enjoy while hot.

Prime Rib With Garlic

Ingredients:

- 2 tsp salt

- 2 tbsp olive oil

- 10 cloves garlic, minced

- 2 tsp dried thyme

- 2 tsp ground black pepper

- 1 piece of 10lb prime rib roast

Directions:

1. In a roasting pan, place roast on with the fatty side up.
2. Mix together thyme, pepper, salt, olive oil, and garlic in a small bowl.
3. Rub the herb mixture all over the roast, and let it sit at room temperature for an hour.
4. Then, preheat the oven to 500°F.
5. For twenty minutes, bake the rib roast on high fire to seal in the juice.
6. Lessen the temperature to 325°F and cool rib roast for 60-75 minutes. Ribs are done once internal temperature of roast has risen to 135°F.
7. Remove roast from oven, and let it rest for 10-15 minutes to retain its juice.
8. Carve the meat, serve, and enjoy.

Chicken Meatballs

Ingredients:

- 1 egg, large
- Spices: legitimate salt, ground pepper and garlic powder
- 2 tbsp. of grain, oat
- 3 tbsp. of hacked dill or parsley
- 1 lb. of chicken, ground
- 1 hacked onion, small
- 1 minced clove of garlic, small

Directions:

1. Preheat stove to 350F.
2. Mince garlic and onion.

3. Add all fixings to enormous bowl. Combine them as one well.
4. Form the combination into 15 to 20 balls and put on a pan.
5. Bake in the center rack of 350F stove for 1820 minutes, till juices are running clear.
6. Remove from broiler and serve.

Limekissed Shrimp

Ingredients:

- 1/2 squeezed lime
- 2 smidgens of salt, kosher
- 3/4 tsp. of pepper, dark, ground
- 28 prepared to cook shrimp, large
- 2 tbsp. of slashed onion

Directions:

1. Spray a skillet with nonstick shower. Heat it over prescription. heat.
2. Add the fixings. Cook till onions and shrimp are finished. Serve.

Oat Bran Galette

Ingredients:

- Plain nonfat greek yogurt
- Nonfat ricotta cheese
- Vanilla
- Cinnamon
- Nutmeg
- Oat bran
- Truvia sweetener
- Egg white

Directions:

1. Combine all dry ingredients in small bowl.

2. Combine egg white, yogurt and ricotta in a bowl and beath until smooth.
3. Combine ingredients and mix until smooth.
4. Bake like regular pancake.
5. I often add cinnamon, nutmeg and vanilla for a sweet but low fat and high protein snack. You can also make a savory version by adding fresh herbs or onions.

Quiche

Ingredients:

- 4 eggs
- 7 oz nonfat cottage cheese
- 1 c chopped onion
- 1 cup diced lean ham
- Salt/Pepper to taste
- Fresh Basil (optional)

Directions:

1. Mix ingredients together and pour into a greased 9 inch pie plate

Cheese And Garlic Chicken Pocket

Ingredients:

- 2 chicken breasts

- Salt, kosher

- 4 tbsp. fatfree cream cheese

Directions:

1. Preheat oven to 350F.
2. Slice chicken breasts in middle area. Create pockets. Don't slice completely through.
3. Sprinkle garlic powder and kosher salt as desired inside pockets created in step 2.
4. Spread aluminum foil in roasting tray. It should be of sufficient size to put chicken breasts inside and wrap meat.
5. Place 1 to 2 tbsp. of cream cheese in pockets. Add additional garlic powder, if desired. Seal

meat up using your fingers. Sprinkle parsley over the top.
6. Cover all with foil and close it up. Cook in 350F oven for 1/2 hour.
7. Open foil. Set oven to grill. Cook for 10 to 15 more minutes and serve.

Cheesy Broccoli Casserole

Ingredients:

- 1 c. milk

- ½ tsp. pepper, black, ground

- 10 oz. cream of mushroom soup, condensed

- 6 oz. crispy fried onions

- 2 c. cheddar cheese shreds

- 2 lb. cooked to tendercrisp, welldrained broccoli florets

Directions:

1. Preheat the oven to 350F. Mix the milk, pepper and soup in a large sized bowl.
2. Add 1 cup fried onions, 1 cup of cheese and the broccoli. Toss and coat gently.

3. Spoon the mixture in 9x13" greased baking dish. Cover dish with aluminum foil.
4. Bake for ½ hour. Remove the foil and stir fully. Sprinkle on the rest of the fried onions and cheese.
5. Leave uncovered and bake for 512 minutes, till onions become a golden brown and the cheese gets bubbly. Serve.

Super Breakfast Smoothie

Ingredients:

- 1 packet milk chocolate instant breakfast mix

- 6 oz. yogurt, strawberry

- ½ c. strawberries, frozen and whole

- 1 c. milk, fatfree

Directions:

1. Place all the Ingredients: in food processor. Blend for a minute till smooth.
2. Serve.

Mushroom Tart

Ingredients:

- 1 small green bell pepper, seeds removed, chopped into very small pieces

- 1 zucchini, chopped into very small pieces

- 4 large button mushrooms, chopped into very small pieces

- 1 small onion, chopped into very small pieces

- ⅛ teaspoon vegetable oil

- 3 eggs

- 2 cups fatfree milk

- 2 teaspoons active dry yeast

- Salt and freshly ground black pepper

Directions:

1. Preheat oven to 450°F. Add the oil to a 9 × 9inch baking dish, using a paper towel to coat it and to wipe out any excess.
2. In a medium bowl, whisk together the eggs, milk, and yeast, plus salt and pepper to taste. Let it sit for 5 minutes.
3. Add the bell pepper, zucchini, mushrooms, and onion. Pour the egg mixture into the prepared baking dish.
4. Bake until set, about 40 minutes.

Vegetable Tart

Ingredients:

- 1 tablespoon chopped fresh herbs, singly or mixed, such as basil, parsley, and rosemary

- 2¼ cups fatfree milk

- 1 cup chopped mixed vegetables, such as tomatoes, zucchini, broccoli, eggplant, and carrots, with all stems removed

- ⅛ teaspoon vegetable oil

- 4 eggs

- A pinch of ground nutmeg

- Salt and freshly ground black pepper

Directions:

1. Preheat oven to 350°F.
2. Add the oil to a 9 × 9inch baking dish, using a paper towel to coat it and to wipe out any excess.
3. In a medium bowl, combine the eggs, nutmeg, herbs, and milk, Add the vegetables, fill the prepared baking dish with the egg mixture.

4. Place the dish into a larger baking dish and fill the larger dish halfway with cold water and bake for 30 minutes.

Date Paste

Ingredients:

- 4 cups pitted dates

- 2 cups water

Directions:

1. Cover dates with boiling water and allow to sit for at least 30 minutes.
2. Drain reserving 2 cups of the soaking water.
3. In a highpowered blender, blend dates and the soaking water on high for a few minutes until it becomes a paste. Add more water if it's difficult to blend or too thick
4. Store paste in a covered glass jar and refrigerate for up to 3 months or longer.

Lemon Cornbread With Strawberries And Cream

Ingredients:

- 1 lb organic strawberries hulled and sliced

- 1 tablespoon sugar *(optional) use cane, Sucanat or coconut sugar

- Strawberries

Cashew cream

- 23 tablespoons maple syrup

- 1 teaspoon vanilla extract

- 1 cup raw cashews

Cake

- 1/2 teaspoon salt

- 1/2 cup applesauce

- 1/4 cup lemon juice

- 1/2 cup nondairy milk

- 1/4 cup maple syrup

- 2 tablespoons ground flaxseeds

- 6 tablespoons water

- 1/2 cup unbleached allpurpose flour

- 1 cup mediumgrind cornmeal

- 1/2 cup blanched almond flour (or use unbleached flour)

- 4 tsp baking powder

Directions:

Strawberries

1. If using sugar to create juicy strawberries, add them to a bowl with 1 tablespoon sugar. Set them aside in the refrigerators for about 10 minutes for them to become juicy.
2. Cashew Cream
3. To quicksoak the cashews, pour boiling water over them and let them sit for 10 minutes. Then, add to a blender with 3/4 cup nondairy milk, vanilla, and maple syrup and blend until smooth. Remove to a container and refrigerate covered until ready to use.

Cake

4. Preheat oven to 400 degrees. Spray a 8 x 8" baking pan sprayed with cooking spray or line with parchment paper.
5. Mix the ground flaxseeds and water in a small bowl and let sit for a few minutes while you prepare the dry ingredients.

6. In a large bowl, blend the dry Ingredients: unbleached flour, almond flour, cornmeal, sugar, baking powder, and salt.
7. In another bowl, combine the nondairy milk, applesauce, lemon juice, maple syrup, and the flax mixture.
8. Mix the dry and wet ingredients together just until moistened.
9. Pour into your prepared 8 x 8" baking pan.
10. Bake at 400 degrees for about 2025 minutes or until the cornbread is started to brown and bounces back when touched on top. Be careful not to overcook as it can become dry.
11. Divide the cake into 6 servings, top with strawberries and a couple of dollops of cashew cream.

Rosemary And Garlic Chicken

Ingredients:

- 2 skinless chicken breasts, diced

- 2 tablespoons Dijon mustard

- 3 cloves fresh garlic, mincedand

- 1 to 2 onions, diced

- 1/8 cup lemon juice

- Rosemary to taste.

Directions:

1. After heating a nonstick pan, cook the garlic in followed by the rosemary. Add in the chicken, ½ cup of water, lemon juice, Dijon mustard and some salt and pepper.
2. When the chicken is cooked, mix in the diced onions and cook until they become tender.
3. Enjoy!

Skewed Lemon Chicken With Dip

Ingredients:

- 3 large chicken breasts.

For the marinade:

- 1 large clove of garlic, sliced

- 1 centimeter cube of fresh ginger, sliced

- A handful of fresh coriander, chopped

- Juice of 1 large lemon

- 1 red chili, cut into small pieces

For the dip:

- 2 tablespoons fresh parsley, chopped

- 250 grams 0% fat Greek yogurtand

- ½ teaspoon paprika

- 2 tablespoons fresh chives, chopped

- Salt and pepper.

Directions:

1. After mixing all the marinade Ingredients: in a bowl, slice the chicken breasts into chunks and mix with the marinade to coat well. Leave the chicken in the bowl to marinate and cover with cling film. Refrigerate for at least 1 hour for best results.
2. While marinating the chicken in the fridge, you can make the dip by mixing together all the Ingredients: in a bowl and season with salt and pepper according to taste. Set aside in the fridge.
3. After marinating, arrange the chicken pieces on skewers and grill for 25 minutes or until the meat is cooked through.

4. Enjoy with the dill and parsley dip!

Multiflavored Beef Attack

Ingredients:

- ½ bunch green onions with tops, chopped
- 1 teaspoon lemongrass
- 1/2 teaspoon garlic, minced
- ¼ cup red onions
- 1 teaspoon red pepper flakes
- A pinch of Stevia
- 8 ounces lean beef
- 1 teaspoon Chinese 5spice
- ½ teaspoon ginger

- ½ teaspoon Thai fish sauce

Directions:

1. Except for the green and red onions, mix together all the Ingredients: in a nonreactive baking dish and in it, marinate the beef for at least 1 hour in the fridge.
2. Heat a nonstick pan and sear the red onions in it for 1 minute. Mix in the beef and sear until medium cooked. Mix in the green onions and stir until hot.
3. Enjoy!

Octopus Salad With Cherry Tomatoes And Arugula

Ingredients:

- 100 g of arugula

- Lemon juice

- Extra virgin olive oil

- 500 g of octopus

- 250 g of cherry tomatoes

- Salt and pepper

- Fresh parsley (optional, for garnish).

Directions:

1. Start by cleaning and preparing the octopus. You can ask your fishmonger to clean it for

you, or you can do it yourself. Remove the octopus head and its internal organs. Rinse the octopus well under cold water.
2. Bring a pot of salted water to a boil. When the water reaches a boil, immerse the octopus for a few seconds and take it out. Repeat this 3 more times. This will help make it more tender when cooking.
3. Boil the salted water and put the octopus in the pot. Cook it over medium heat for about 4050 minutes, or until the octopus is tender. You can check the cooking by inserting the tip of a knife into the octopus: if it goes in easily, it's ready.
4. Drain it and let it cool. Once cooled, cut the octopus into smaller pieces, as you prefer.
5. In a bowl, add the halved cherry tomatoes, arugula and octopus pieces.
6. Prepare the salad dressing. In a small bowl, mix the lemon juice, extra virgin olive oil, salt

and pepper to taste. Stir well to emulsify the sauce.
7. Pour the sauce over the octopus, cherry tomatoes and arugula salad. Stir gently to distribute the dressing evenly.
8. You can garnish the salad with chopped fresh parsley or whole leaves for an eyecatching presentation.
9. Let the salad rest in the refrigerator for at least 30 minutes to let the flavors meld.
10. Serve the octopus salad with cherry tomatoes and arugula as an appetizer or light main course. It's perfect for a fresh and healthy summer dinner.
11. Remember to adjust portions according to your dietary needs and specific Dukan Diet guidelines.

Eggplant Rolls With Cooked Ham And Cheese

Ingredients:

- 200 g of cheese (for example, mozzarella or provola)
- 400 ml of tomato puree
- 1 clove of garlic
- Extra virgin olive oil
- Salt and pepper
- 2 eggplants
- 4 slices of cooked ham
- Fresh basil (optional, for garnish).

Directions:

1. Start by cutting off the ends of the eggplants and peel them. Then cut them lengthwise, obtaining thin slices about 0.5 cm thick.
2. Put the eggplant slices on a cutting board and salt them on both sides. Let them sit for about 15 minutes to remove excess water.
3. Meanwhile, prepare the tomato sauce. In a pan, heat a drizzle of olive oil and add the whole garlic clove. Sauté the garlic for a few minutes, then remove it from the pan. Add the tomato puree, salt and pepper to taste. Simmer over mediumlow heat for about 1015 minutes, until the sauce thickens slightly. Season with salt and pepper, if necessary.
4. Rinse the eggplant slices under running water to remove the salt and carefully dry them with paper towels.
5. Take a slice of eggplant and place a slice of cooked ham and some cheese on the widest part of the slice. Gently roll the eggplant

around the ham and cheese, forming a roll. Repeat this with all the eggplant slices.

6. Arrange the eggplant rolls in a baking tray lightly greased with olive oil. Pour the tomato sauce on the surface of the rolls.
7. Bake in a preheated oven at 180°C for about 2530 minutes, or until the eggplants are soft and lightly browned.
8. If you want a touch of crunch, you can sprinkle the surface of the rolls with a little grated cheese and grate them in the oven for a few minutes before serving.
9. You can garnish the eggplant rolls with cooked ham and cheese with fresh basil leaves for a touch of freshness.
10. Serve the eggplant rolls as a second course accompanied by a side dish of vegetables or a fresh salad.

11. Be sure to adjust portions according to your dietary needs and specific Dukan Diet guidelines.

Turkey Skewers With Peppers And Courgettes

Ingredients:

- 2 medium courgettes cut into rounds

- Juice of 1 lemon

- 2 tablespoons of olive oil

- Salt and pepper

- Spices to taste (for example, paprika, oregano, thyme)

- 500 g of turkey breast cut into cubes

- 2 bell peppers (preferably of different colors) cut into cubes

- 46 wooden or metal skewers.

Directions:

1. Start by preparing the marinade. In a bowl, mix the lemon juice, olive oil, salt, pepper and any spices to taste. Adjust seasonings according to your tastes.
2. Add the turkey cubes to the marinade and mix well to make sure they are completely covered in the marinade. Cover the bowl and leave to marinate in the refrigerator for at least 30 minutes, but preferably a couple of hours to get the most intense flavor.
3. Meanwhile, prepare the vegetables. Cut the peppers into cubes and the courgettes into slices.

4. Once the turkey has marinated enough, alternately thread the cubes of turkey, peppers, and courgettes onto the skewers.
5. Heat a grill or nonstick skillet. Lightly brush the skewers with a little olive oil to prevent sticking.
6. Cook the kebabs on the grill or in the skillet over mediumhigh heat for about 10 to 12 minutes, turning occasionally, until the turkey is cooked through and the vegetables are tender and lightly browned.
7. Once cooked, you can serve the turkey skewers with peppers and courgettes as a second course, accompanied by a side dish of vegetables or a fresh salad.
8. Remember to adjust portions according to your dietary needs and specific Dukan Diet guidelines.

Pan Fried Trout

Ingredients:

- ½ lemon

- Salt, to taste

- ½ trout

- ½ bay leaf

- Pepper, to taste

Directions:

1. Clean and gut the fish – ensure it remains whole. (If you wish, remove only the head.)
2. Cut the lemon into half – then keep one aside. (This means you have two quarters of a lemon.)
3. Take one quarter, and squeeze the juice from it all over the fish, and into the cavity.

4. Cut the other quarter into half and place both of the resultant pieces in the cavity of the fish, along with the bay leaf.
5. Season using salt and pepper according to your taste.
6. Cook the fish on a pan, turning it over to let both sides cook whenever necessary.

Salade Nicoise

Ingredients:

- 5 tbsp capers

- LemonDijon dressing (Specified below)

- Fresh dill, to garnish

- 2 hardboiled eggs, cut into quarters

- 2 cans of tuna, packed

- 7 scallions, chopped

For the dressing

- 6 tbsp fresh lemon juice

- 4 tsp fresh thyme

- 2 garlic cloves, crushed

- 6 tbsp fatfree yogurt

- 6 tbsp Dijon mustard

Directions:

1. To prepare the dressing, add the garlic cloves, yogurt, mustard, lemon juice and thyme to a food processor. Blend till the resultant dressing is smooth in consistency.
2. Next, drain the canned tuna and using a fork, make chunks of it.
3. Arrange the tuna in a shallow dish. Next, place the quartered eggs on it.
4. Similarly, place the capers and the scallions on the salad. Serve alongside the lemonDijon dressing you made earlier.

Chicken Bruschetta

Ingredients:

- 1 ripe tomato, diced
- 1 tablespoon light mayonnaise
- 1 teaspoon mustard
- Lettuce or arugula for garnish (optional)
- 2 slices of whole wheat or rye bread
- 150 g cooked chicken breast, diced
- Salt and pepper to taste.

Directions:

1. Toast the bread slices in the toaster oven or under the oven grill. In a bowl, mix diced chicken, diced tomato, light mayonnaise, and mustard.

2. Season with salt and pepper to taste. Spread the chicken mixture over the toasted bread slices.
3. Garnish with lettuce or arugula leaves (if desired). Serve the chicken bruschetta as an appetizer.

Shrimp And Avocado Salad

Ingredients:

- Green salad mix to taste

- Lemon juice

- Extra virgin olive oil

- 200 g shelled shrimp

- 1 ripe avocado, diced

- Salt and pepper to taste.

Directions:

1. Heat a nonstick skillet over mediumhigh heat. Add shelled shrimp to the skillet and cook for 23 minutes per side, until pink and fully cooked.

2. In a bowl, mix the cooked shrimp, diced avocado, green salad mix, lemon juice, extra virgin olive oil, salt, and pepper.
3. Mix all Ingredients: well until evenly mixed. Serve the shrimp and avocado salad cold.

Ham And Cheese Rolls

Ingredients:

- 8 slices of ham
- 100 g sliced cheese
- (such as provolone or mozzarella)
- Arugula or spinach for garnish (optional)

Directions:

1. Arrange a slice of prosciutto on a cutting board or work surface. Place a slice of cheese on the slice of ham.
2. Add a few leaves of arugula or spinach on top of the cheese slice (if desired). Roll the ham around the cheese and arugula, creating a small roll.
3. Repeat the process with the remaining slices of ham and cheese.

4. Cut each roll in half or into smaller pieces. Serve the ham and cheese rolls as an appetizer.

Blanched Brussel Sprouts With Crispy Ham

Ingredients:

- 2 ½ lbs brussel sprouts

- Handful fresh sage, shredded

- 3 slices lean ham, sliced thin

Directions:

1. Bring pot of salted water to boil, and blanch the sprouts for about 3 minutes. Drain the sprouts and place in a bowl filled with ice cold water.
2. Once cooled, drain and set sprouts aside. Cut ham into 1" strips, and fry in nonstick pan until crispy.
3. Add sprouts to ham and fry for a continued 23 minutes. Sprinkle with sage.

Dilled Fish Cakes

Ingredients:

- 2 salmon fillets, cut into small pieces

- 1 tbsp. dried dill

- Juice from half a lemon

- 2 tbsp. fatfree yogurt

- 2 spring onions, chopped finely

- 1 1" cube ginger, grated

- Olive oil cooking spray

Directions:

1. Combine onions, ginger, and salmon into a bowl. Add dill, and mix well.
2. Separate mixture into fourths. Squeeze each into a ball, and shape into a fish cake.
3. Combine yogurt and lemon juice. Serve as dipping sauce with fish cakes.

Butterfinger Pie

Ingredients:

- ¼ cup peanut butter

- 1 cup powdered sugar (to decorate)

- 2 cups butterfinger candy bars

- Pastry sheets

- 1 package cream cheese

- 1 tsp vanilla extract

- 8 oz whipped topping

Directions:

1. Line a pie plate or pie form with pastry and cover the edges of the plate depending on your preference

2. In a bowl combine all pie Ingredients: together and mix well
3. Pour the mixture over the pastry
4. Bake at 400425 F for 2530 minutes or until golden brown
5. When ready remove from the oven and let it rest for 15 minutes

Watermelon Smoothie

Ingredients:

- 1 cup vanilla yogurt
- 2 tablespoons maple syrup
- 1 cup ice
- 2 cups watermelon
- 1 cup almond milk

Directions:

1. In a blender place all Ingredients: and blend until smooth
2. Pour smoothie in a glass and serve

Chocolate Pralines

Ingredients:

- 2 tbsp skimmed milk
- 7 tbsp skimmed milk powder (think this cud be reduced....)
- 3 tbsp sweetener
- 1 tbsp coco powder
- 1 egg yolk
- 8 drops vanilla essence

Directions:

1. Mix the lot together and using a teaspoon put them onto tin foil then pass into wee paper cups, or direct onto a plate.
2. Put in fridge to set.

Sweet & Sour Chicken

Ingredients:

- 3 TBSP reduced sugar ketchup (i reckon u cud get away with passata)
- 3 TBSP sweetener
- 1/4 cup white vinegar
- 1 cup of chicken or vegetable stock.
- 1 clove garlic
- 2 TBSP soy sauce

Directions:

1. 'Fry' off chicken chunks, mushrooms, onions, peppers (i use a LARGE frying pan)
2. In a mixing bowl mix together then add to the cooked chicken mix.

3. In a cup mix 2 TBSP cornflour (tolerated item) with a bit of cold water stir this into the liquid/chicken mix in your frying pan continue to stir and the mix should thicken a bit.
4. Leave to bubble away nicely to cook off the vinegar for 5 or so mins. IT SMELLS LUSH.

Steak Pizzaola

Ingredients:

- DD friendly tomato sauce

- 1/4 cup shredded fat free mozerella cheese

- 1 steak for each serving I used New York Strip

- 1/2 green pepper, 1/2 small onion and 4 or 5 white mushrooms for each steak

For the sauce:

- 1/2 tsp dried oregano

- 1/2 tsp dried basil

- freshly ground pepper to taste

- 1 large can diced tomatoes (28 oz.)

- 1 large can plain tomato sauce (28 oz.)

- 1/2 cup finely dice onion

- 3 cloves minced garlic

Directions:

1. Mix all sauce Ingredients: together in medium saucepan, simmer over medium heat for 30 40 minutes
2. While the sauce is simmering, slice the peppers, onions and mushrooms and saute them in a pan seasoned with nonstick cooking spray. Saute until veggies are crisptender.
3. Heat grill and when the grill is good and hot, sear the steaks on one side, Cook about 7 minutes for medium.
4. Flip the steaks over and place the pepper, onion and mushroom mixture carefully on top. Ladel on about 3/4 cup of tomatoe sauce over the veggies. Sprinkle on the cheese and close the grill cover. Continue grilling about 45 more minutes.

5. Carefully remove steaks to a serving dish with a wide spatula.

Regularity Muffins

Ingredients:

- 1/2 tsp bicarbonate of soda

- 1 tsp baking powder

- 1 pinch salt

- 140g (1cup) oat bran

- 35g (1/2 cup) wheat bran

- 40g (1/4 cup) linseed/flaxseed (ground in coffee grinder to release more nutrients, or left whole to reduce calories)

- 250ml (1 cup) buttermilk, or sweet milk acidulated with 1 tsp vinegar or lemon juice

Directions:

1. Preheat oven to 200oC / 400oF
2. If you don't have buttermilk on hand, stir vinegar or lemon juice into ordinary milk and set aside to sour while you are preparing the dry Ingredients:.
3. Weigh or measure oat bran, wheat bran and flaxseed/linseed into a mixing bowl.
4. Rub bicarbonate of soda between palms over the bowl, or sift, to ensure there aren't any clumps which would taste foul.
5. Add baking powder and salt, mix thoroughly.
6. Prepare 8 muffin tins (silicone are easiest to unmould and don't need greasing).
7. Add buttermilk or acidulated milk to dry ingredients, mix thoroughly but quickly. Don't overwork.
8. Speed is of the essence here because the acid in the milk activates the bicarbonate of soda and makes bubbles which lighten the muffinsif you wait too long it will lose this

effect. Distribute evenly among 8 muffin tins and bake immediately for 20'.
9. Leave in tin on rack for a few minutes before unmoulding.
10. One muffin is daily oat bran requirement and wheat bran tolerance on Dukan Diet.
Keeps for over a week in tupper ware container or plastic bag in fridge, can be reheated in toaster or microwave.
11. If you used whole flaxseed/linseed chew well to break them so you get benefit of some of their omega oil.

Baked Bass

Ingredients:

- 2 tomatoes, cut in ½
- 1 lemon, cut into slices
- A handful of fresh parsley, finely chopped 1 clove of garlic, crushed through a garlic press
- 2 fresh bass fish fillets
- 2 onions, peeled and sliced into strips
- Salt and pepper

Directions:

1. Preheat the oven to 375 F.
2. Lay the onions onto an oven proof baking dish. Lay the bass fillets on top of the onions, and surround with the cut tomatoes.

3. Lay the lemon slices over the fillets with any remaining around the fish with the tomatoes. Sprinkle the tomatoes with the herbs and crushed garlic, and season with salt and pepper.
4. Bake for 20-30 minutes or until the meat has turned white, checking close to the end time to ensure the fish does not overcook.

Suitable Protein Patty Soup

Ingredients:

- 2 large egg (s)

- 2 tablespoon bran, (oat), easily soluble flakes

- 50 ml milk, 1.5%

- 1 pinch (s) salt

- 10 g broth, instant

- 1 liter water

- 3 drops olive oil

Directions:

1. Bring the water and stock powder to the boil together.

2. Dissolve the oat bran in the milk in a container. Add the eggs and whisk everything together. Add the salt.
3. Let a pan rubbed with a few drops of oil (add 34 drops of oil to the pan and rub the whole thing with a paper towel) warm up.
4. Slowly cook the Flädle mixture in the pan it should ideally be golden brown on both sides. Turning it around is a bit difficult, but Flädle naturally forgives small mistakes, they will be cut up anyway.
5. Let the pancake cool briefly and then cut into strips (the length of the strips can be adjusted to personal preference). Add the pancakes to the soup and enjoy.
6. Tip for turning: I use two dough scrapers at the same time. Because this type of pancake loves to break.
7. The best chance of turning it whole or at least in half is with several scrapers.

8. Info: for the sake of simplicity, I use soup powder (but in homeopathic dilution because of the fat and salt). For Dukan fans: the recipe is also suitable for the attack phase.
9. You just have to pay attention to the fat and salt because of the broth but the soup is the most important thing.
10. For Dukan newbies: the diet is about not eating any carbohydrates (after an initial phase, they are allowed again every other day in the form of vegetables, but of course no potatoes or the like) the diet is therefore only for real meat and suitable for yoghurt lovers.

Endive And Caviar Salad

Ingredients:

- 1 tablespoon lumpfish or salmon roe
- 1 tablespoon white wine vinegar
- 2 heads of endive
- ¼ cup fatfree sour cream

Directions:

1. Slice the endive down the middle and then again across.
2. Place the leaves into a salad bowl.
3. For the dressing: mix the sour cream, caviar, and vinegar.
4. Toss the dressing with the endives.

Easy Seafood Stirfry

Ingredients:

- ½ pound bay scallops or halved sea scallops

- ¼ pound medium raw shrimp, peeled and deveined 2 cloves of garlic, minced

- 2 cups of green beans

- ¼ cup of thinly sliced green onions

- "2 packs of Dukan Diet Shirataki rice

- 1 ounce of dried shiitake mushrooms or 1.5 cups of fresh mushrooms

- ½ cup of fatfree, low sodium chicken broth

- 1 tablespoon low sodium soy sauce

- 4.5 teaspoons of cornstarch (tolerated)

- 1 teaspoon olive oil, divided (tolerated)

Directions:

1. Prepare Shirataki rice according to package instructions and set aside.
2. Place mushrooms in small bowlcover with boiling water.
3. Soak 20 minutes to soften. Drainsqueeze out excess water. Discard stemsslice
4. caps.
5. Blend broth and soy sauce into cornstarch in another small bowl until smoothset aside.
6. Heat ½ teaspoon oil in wok or skillet over medium heat. Add scallops,
7. shrimp and garlicstirfry 3 minutes or until seafood is opaque.
8. Remove and reserve.
9. Add remaining ½ teaspoon oil to wok. Add mushrooms and green beans
10. stirfry 3 minutes or until green beans are crisptender.

11. Stir broth mixtureadd to wok. Cook and stir 2 minutes or until sauce boils and thickens. Return seafood and any accumulated juices to wokcook and stir until heated through. Sprinkle with green onions.
12. Plate with the Shirataki rice.

Tea Cake With Goji Berries According

INGREDIENTS:

- 4 tbsp cornstarch80 gr4 dops

- 2 tbsp olive oilor any vegetable

- 2 tbsp dried goji berries

- 3 tbsp sugarfree syrup with berry flavorwhich can be heated

- 1 tsp baking powder

- 1/3 tsp ground cinnamon

- 250 ml. Strong teawarm not hot

- 4 tbsp oat bran60 gr

- 3 tbsp wheat gluten75 gr

- Vanillin or aromatic "cupcake" or "biscuit"

- Sucrose

Directions:

1. Dukan's gingerbread is prepared without the hassle!
2. At the beginning of cooking, soak the goji berries in a small amount of warm water. Not hot!
3. Let's leave it for 35 minutes.
4. After the time has passed, drain the water from the berries. We squeeze the berries.
5. Add syrup to berries.
6. If you don't have syrup, no problem! Replace it with 34 tbsp. a spoonful of mineral water with a few drops of any berry flavor (cherry, strawberry, raspberry, etc.)
7. We grind the berries with a blender to the state of "jam" pieces of berries should remain

8. Now let's prepare the dough for Dukan's gingerbread. Add all dry Ingredients: to the bowl.
9. We mix everything until smooth. All dough Ingredients: are ready.
10. Add the tea leaves, goji and 2 tbsp to the bulk Ingredients:. olive oil. Mix with a mixer until smooth.
11. The dough turns out to be an interesting consistency a little viscous. This is how it should be
12. Spread the dough evenly into the mold.
13. It is better to choose a shape with a small diameter (I have 18 cm), otherwise you will get not a gingerbread but a pancake
14. We put in an oven preheated to 180 C.
15. We bake without convection! If your stove only bakes on convection mode, reduce the temperature to 160 C

16. Bake for 25-30 minutes depending on your shape.
17. We check the readiness with a toothpick (there should be no traces of dough on it)
18. Take the mold out of the oven immediately. Place the Ducane cake on a wire rack and cover with a clean kitchen towel.
19. Cool down completely.
20. It turns out a wonderful lean pastry according to Dukan!
21. The casserole is flavorful and juicy! After a few days, it does not even get stale if stored in a regular paper bag or parchment.

Muesli Bars In "White Chocolate"

Ingredients:

- 2 tbsp. l. goji berries

- sucrose

- any nutty or fruity flavor(if there is)

- 1 egg

- 4 tbsp oat bran60 gr

- 60 ml. skimmed milk (liquid)(0.5%1.5%)

- 56 tbsp catfish (skimmed milk powder)60 gr   (2 DOPs)

- 2 tsp sesame10 gr(according to the norm of oil, for 2 days)

- 2 tsp flax seed10 gr

For glaze

- 120 ml. skimmed milk (liquid)(0.5%1.5%)
- 56 tbsp COM60 gr(2 DOPs)
- sucrose
- Aromic "Chocolate" or "Cocoa Beans"

Directions:

1. We spread the milk powder for the muesli itself in a dry frying pan and fry over a very low heat until golden brown. Stir constantly. We try to break the formed lumps. When the milk is fried, it must be crushed again. I do this with a coffee grinder.
2. Soak the goji berries inside warm water for 5 minutes. Drain the water, squeeze the berries.
3. Add milk to oat bran. We mix. And leave the bran to swell for 510 minutes. During this time, the bran will absorb all the moisture.
4. In the swollen bran, add all the dry Ingredients: and soaked goji berries.
5. Let's mix everything. It turns out dry crumb
6. Now add egg and aroma to the mixture. Mix everything with your hands you get a thick mass. If dry, add a tablespoon of liquid milk.

7. Place a silicone mat or use parchment paper on a baking sheet. Using a wide spatula or a wide kitchen knife, spread the mass evenly.
8. Choose the thickness as you wish the size of future bars will depend on the thickness. The thinner the mass is, the crispier the muesli bars will turn out.
9. To compact the mass better, you can press down a little on top with a cutting board.
10. With a sharp knife we outline future bars (I got 6 large bars)
11. We do not cut through the mass to the end!
12. We heat the oven to 160180C. We bake our muesli bars for 2030 minutes depending on the size (We bake on the mode without convection!)
13. Bake for 1015 minutes, then turn over and bake for another 1015 minutes.

14. The goji berries in the bars may start to get very dark or even burn then cover the mass with foil.
15. We take it out of the oven and cut the still warm mass according to the preliminary outlines into bars.
16. Even when the mass for the bars themselves is baked, we will make the icing. Mixing all the Ingredients:
17. We mix them until smooth (preferably with a mixer), so that no lumps remain. Leave the glaze in the refrigerator, it will thicken a little.
18. Ready bars are still warm! Cover with plenty of frosting. On warm bars, the icing will absorb more evenly and harden faster.
19. It's better to cover the icing on the grate
20. Ready muesli bars are sent to the refrigerator. The icing should be completely dry and not smeared.

21. Now these Dukan muesli bars can be taken out of the refrigerator and stored, for example, in a tin.
22. Try these wonderful Dukan muesli bars! Delicious, healthy and nutritious bars! And how convenient it is to take them with you!

Easy Herb Roasted Turkey

Ingredients:

- 2 teaspoons dried basil
- 1 teaspoon ground sage
- 1 teaspoon salt
- ½ teaspoon black pepper
- 1 (12 pound) whole turkey
- ¾ cup olive oil
- 2 tablespoons garlic powder
- 2 cups water

Directions:

1. Preheat oven to 325 degrees F (165 degrees C). Clean turkey (discard giblets and organs), and place in a roasting pan with a lid.
2. In a small bowl, combine olive oil, garlic powder, dried basil, ground sage, salt, and black pepper.
3. Using a basting brush, apply the mixture to the outside of the uncooked turkey. Pour water into the bottom of the roasting pan, and cover.
4. Bake for 3 to 3 1/2 hours, or until the internal temperature of the thickest part of the thigh measures 180 degrees F (82 degrees C).
5. Remove bird from oven, and allow to stand for about 30 minutes before carving.

Roasted Okra

Ingredients:

- 1 tablespoon olive oil

- 2 teaspoons kosher salt, or to taste

- 18 eaches fresh okra pods, sliced 1/3 inch thick

- 2 teaspoons black pepper, or to taste

Directions:

1. Preheat an oven to 425 degrees F (220 degrees C).
2. Arrange the okra slices in one layer on a foil lined cookie sheet.
3. Drizzle with olive oil and sprinkle with salt and pepper. Bake in the preheated oven for 10 to 15 minutes.

Pak Choi And Chicken Stirfry

Ingredients:

- 1 bunch scallions/Spring onions cut into 1" slices

- 1/2 cup chicken stock

- 3 tablespoons of soy sauce

- 2 teaspoons of cornstarch/cornflour

- 4 teaspoons of rapeseed oil

- 1 tablespoon finely diced garlic

- 1 lb cooked chicken breast pulled apart into small bite size pieces

- 2 finely sliced Pak Choi with the green leaves and white stalks kept apart

- 10 ounces sliced mushrooms
- 1 cup carrots batons (1/4 " thick)
- 1 tablespoon finely diced ginger

Directions:

1. Mix the chicken stock, soy sauce and cornstarch/cornflour in a small jug with a whisk.
2. Heat the rapeseed oil in a large skillet or wok over mediumhigh heat. It is best not to use olive oil as if you're not careful you can burn it.
3. Add the stalks of the Pak Choi, carrots and mushrooms and cook until the carrots are just tender. This will be around 5 minutes.
4. Add the garlic and ginger and a couple of minutes later add the chicken and scallions/Spring onions.

5. After a couple more minutes add the Pak Choi leaves and stir in before adding the mixture in the jug.
6. Continue stirring until the sauce thickens.
7. Serve at once on a bed of Shirataki noodles.

Quick And Easy Chicken And Tomato

Ingredients:

- 1 and 1/2 cups of chicken stock

- 2 teaspoons of olive oil or rapeseed oil

- 2 tablespoons of balsamic vinegar

- 1 tablespoon of chopped chives

- 2 cups of halved cherry tomatoes

- 8 skinless, boneless chicken thighs or 4 skinless, boneless chicken breasts

- 1/2 cup of diced red onion

- Freshly ground black pepper and sea salt to taste

Directions:

1. On a medium heat fry the onions in the oil in a non stick pan (which has a lid) for a couple of minutes and then add the chicken pieces.
2. Brown the chicken on each side for 5 minutes each side.
3. Add the chicken stock and balsamic vinegar and then mix in the tomatoes and chives.
4. Place a lid on the pan and reduce the heat to a simmer for about 20 minutes until the chicken is cooked through.
5. Take off the lid and continue to cook until the sauce has the desired consistency.
6. Serve with vegetables or Shirataki noodles as desired.

Melt In Your Mouth Baby Back Ribs

Ingredients:

- 1 pinch crushed red pepper

- 1 pinch salt

- 1 pinch black pepper

- 2 bottles of 12oz porter beer, room temperature

- 4 cups barbecue sauce

- 6 lbs pork baby back ribs

Directions:

1. Cut into 23 rib portions, and boil for 20 minutes in a pot of water with crushed red pepper, black pepper, and salt.
2. Drain ribs, and set aside for 30 mins.

3. Preheat outdoor grill to high fire, as you coat the ribs with barbecue sauce.
4. Grill ribs for 8 minutes per side.
5. Remove ribs from grill, and transfer to a slow cooker. Add the bottle of beer and remaining barbecue sauce into a slow cooker, and cook on high for 3 hours.
6. Sauce should cover half of the ribs. Check ribs each hour, and add more beer, if needed, to dilute sauce.
7. Ribs are ready to serve once meat easily falls off the bone.

Dijonworcestershire Marinated Grilled Flank Steak

Ingredients:

- 1 tbsp Dijon mustard

- 1 ½ tbsp Worcestershire sauce

- 2 tbsp fresh lemon juice

- ¼ cup red wine vinegar

- 1/3 cup soy sauce

- 1 ½ lbs flank steak

- ½ tsp ground black pepper

- 2 cloves garlic, minced

- ½ cup vegetable oil

Directions:

1. Thoroughly mix ground black pepper, garlic, mustard, Worcestershire sauce, lemon juice, vinegar, soy sauce, and oil in a medium bowl.
2. Place steak in a shallow glass dish, and pour the marinade over it. Turn meat to coat with marinade, refrigerate for 6 hours, and turn to coat meat every hour.
3. Grease grate, and on mediumhigh fire, preheat.
4. Grill meat for 5 minutes per side, and cook to desired doneness.
5. Serve, and enjoy!

www.ingramcontent.com/pod-product-compliance
Lightning Source LLC
La Vergne TN
LVHW010224070526
838199LV00062B/4713